Sweeter than HONEY
Deuteronomy

A Bible Study Workbook

Jeremy Sweets

Nashville, Tennessee

Sweeter Than Honey Deuteronomy
A Bible Study Workbook

Copyright © 2020 by Jeremy Sweets

Guten Book Publishing
Nashville, Tennessee
gutenbookpub@gmail.com

Latest update: 8/22/2023

All rights reserved. This book or any portion thereof may not be reproduced or used in any manner whatsoever without the express written permission of the publisher except for the use of brief quotations in a book review.

ISBN 13 Number: 978-1-953850-00-3

Scripture quotations are from the ESV® Bible (The Holy Bible, English Standard Version®), copyright © 2001 by Crossway, a publishing ministry of Good News Publishers. Used by permission. All rights reserved.

Printed in the United States of America

Sweeter than HONEY Studies

Sweeter Than Honey Studies examine the Biblical text to highlight its sweetness and encourage discipleship in Christ.

Sweeter Than Honey Deuteronomy
Table of Contents

Lesson 1: Introduction		1

History of the Covenant (Deuteronomy 1-4)

Lesson 2: Historical Review of the Covenant	Deuteronomy 1-3	5
Lesson 3: The Foundation of the Covenant	Deuteronomy 4	11

Principles of the Covenant (Deuteronomy 5-11)

Lesson 4: The Ten Commandments	Deuteronomy 5	17
Lesson 5: Election and Testing	Deuteronomy 6-7	25
Lesson 6: Remember and Do Not Forget	Deuteronomy 8-9	31
Lesson 7: Humble and Devoted Hearts	Deuteronomy 10-11	37

Stipulations of the Covenant (Deuteronomy 12-26)

Lesson 8: The Covenant Laws, Part 1	Deuteronomy 12-26	43
Lesson 9: The Covenant Laws, Part 2	Deuteronomy 12-26	49

Consequences of the Covenant (Deuteronomy 27-28)

Lesson 10: Blessings and Curses	Deuteronomy 27-28	55

The Choice of the Covenant (Deuteronomy 29-30)

Lesson 11: Israel's Choice	Deuteronomy 29-30	61

Continuity of the Covenant (Deuteronomy 31-34)

Lesson 12: Witnesses to the Covenant	Deuteronomy 31-32	67
Lesson 13: The Final Days of Moses	Deuteronomy 33-34	73

Review	79
Resources	83

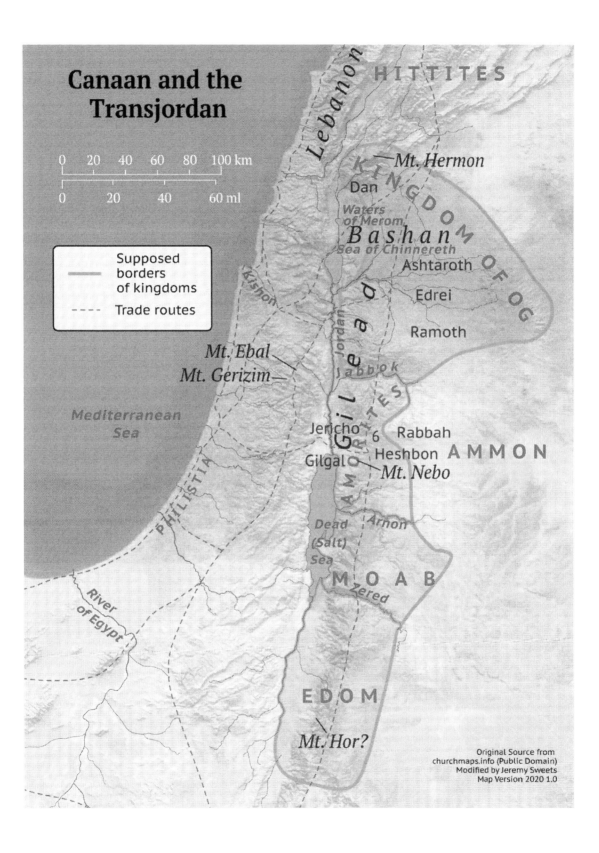

Lesson 1

Introduction

Sweeter Than Honey Deuteronomy

"Second Law"

Deuteronomy is the fifth and final book in the Pentateuch, continuing the narrative account of Israel's journey

The Law at Mt. Sinai	The Law at Moab
Ex. 19 – Num. 10	Deuteronomy

from Egypt to the Promised Land of Canaan. It derives its name from the title given in the Septuagint, the Greek translation of the text, and it means "second law."

The Covenant Law is first given at Mt. Sinai to the generation who escaped Egyptian bondage in the Exodus. After that generation died in the wilderness because of their faithlessness at Kadesh, a new generation continued the journey, coming along the eastern side of Canaan and camping in the Plains of Moab in preparation to enter Canaan. Deuteronomy is a record of the instruction that Moses gave this second generation in Moab.

It repeats many of the laws previously recorded in Exodus, Leviticus and Numbers, but it should not be considered mere repetition. Eugene Merrill states that Deuteronomy "is not a second law but an amplification and advancement of the covenant text first articulated to Moses and Israel at Sinai nearly forty years earlier" (NAC, Deuteronomy, p. 22). This "advancement" results from an application of the law for a new generation in a new land and in a new context. This new context provides issues and challenges that are addressed within the law.

The Setting of the Book (1:1-5)

The opening verses of Deuteronomy pick up where Numbers leaves off, introducing the words of Moses to the people (Num. 36:13; Deut. 1:1). These verses establish the setting of the book, serving as a preamble for Israel's covenant renewal with God. It identifies the parties involved, their location, and the timeframe for the covenant. Similar preambles have been found in other covenant documents from the Ancient Near East.

> These are the commandments and the rules that the LORD commanded through Moses to the people of Israel in the plains of Moab by the Jordan at Jericho (Num. 36:13).
>
> ----------------------------------
>
> These are the words that Moses spoke to all Israel beyond the Jordan in the wilderness... (Deut. 1:1)

Sweeter Than Honey Deuteronomy

Notice that Moses speaks the words that God gives him (v. 1, 3) and explains them (v. 5). *Torah* is the Hebrew word for law, and it includes instruction in addition to regulation.

1. How is instruction different from law? How do the goals of each differ?

2. Identify the missing elements of the setting below.

What?	These are the words that Moses spoke (v. 1) … according to all that the LORD had given him (v. 3)
Who?	Speaker and Recipients:
Where?	
When?	
Why?	God's promise to the fathers (1:6-8)

Authorship

The authorship of Deuteronomy has traditionally been ascribed to Moses, although some people dispute that he wrote the book. The text certainly presents Moses as the mediator of the Law, receiving the Law from God and relaying it to the Israelites in both oral and written form.
- He writes down the law he received in Exodus (Ex. 24:4), including the words of the covenant in the Ten Commandments (Ex. 34:28).
- He records the stages of Israel's journey in the wilderness (Num. 33:1-2).
- He writes the laws found in Deuteronomy (Deut. 31:9).
- He writes down the "Song of Moses" (Deut. 31:22).

The writings of Moses provide the foundational portion of the Pentateuch, particularly the laws. Considering that his death is recorded in Deut. 34, it is likely that other people played at least some role in the writing and development of the books. The final chapter also references an unspecified future time period (34:6, 10).

Moses' Speeches

The book of Deuteronomy serves as a farewell address of Moses to the Israelites before entering the land of Canaan. It can be outlined according to the major speeches that

> **Concentric Structure**
>
> A. Outer Frame: A Look Backward (ch. 1-3)
>   B. Inner Frame: Covenant Preparations (ch. 4-11)
>   C. Central Core: Covenant Stipulations (ch. 12-26)
>   B'. Inner Frame: Covenant Ceremony (ch. 27-30)
> A'. Outer Frame: A Look Forward (ch. 31-34)

Moses makes with a concluding section consisting of smaller units. The speeches follow a natural progression from the history of the people relating to the covenant, the law of the covenant and its importance, and finally a concluding challenge to the people. The book concludes with an epilogue that contains a farewell from Moses in the form of a song and blessing before recording a narrative account of his death and the transition of leadership power to Joshua.

Speech	Scripture	Content	Note
Moses' 1st Speech	1:1-4:43	History of Israel	Introduced by "These are the words" (1:1)
Moses' 2nd Speech	4:44-28:68	The Law	Introduced by "This is the law" (4:44)
Moses' 3rd Speech	29:1-30:20	Summary	Introduced by "These are the words" (29:1)
Epilogue	31:1-34:12	Moses' song, blessing, death & commission of Joshua	Introduction for Song (31:30) and Blessing (33:1)

* Note the heading "these are the laws…" can also be found in 6:1 and 12:1 indicating sections within the 2nd speech.

> **Covenant Format in Deuteronomy**
>
> **Preamble** – setting and occasion of the covenant 1:1-5
> **Historical Prologue** – reminder of ruler's accomplishments 1:6-4:43
> **Stipulations** – laws of the covenant agreement 4:44-26:15
> **Document Clause** – provision for storage of document 27:2-3
> **Witnesses** – those who attest to the covenant's agreement ch. 31-32
> **Blessings & Curses** – consequences for obeying/disobeying ch. 27-28

The Covenant

Deuteronomy is a presentation of the covenant to the second generation of those who departed Egyptian bondage. A covenant is simply an agreement between two parties for peace. It was a common agreement in the Ancient Near East, and it was familiar to Israel, having already made a covenant with God at Mt. Sinai. There are different types of covenants, but the one that most resembles God's covenant with Israel is called a Suzerainty-Vassal covenant, which involved an agreement between parties of unequal standing. The suzerain is the king or superior party who offers some type of blessing or protection to the vassal, the inferior party. In return, the vassal gives his allegiance to the suzerain and commits to follow the covenant stipulations. Suzerainty-Vassal covenants often take a familiar form, which includes a preamble, historical prologue, stipulations, document clause, witnesses to the covenant, and consequences. It often accompanies a ratification ceremony or oath. Deuteronomy contains these elements with the book structured as a covenant document.

The elements of the covenant line up in the following manner within the speeches of Moses:

History of the Covenant	**Principles** of the Covenant	**Stipulations** of the Covenant	**Consequences** of the Covenant	**The Choice** of the Covenant	**Continuity** of the Covenant
Deut. 1-4	**Deut. 5-11**	**Deut. 12-26**	**Deut. 27-28**	**Deut. 29-30**	**Deut. 31-34**
1st Speech	2nd Speech			3rd Speech	Epilogue

Important Themes

Moses' speeches or sermons, as they have sometimes been called, are filled with words of exhortation, encouragement, and warnings. They present many important themes and comprise the dying words of Israel's finest leader.

- ❖ **The Uniqueness of God.** The fundamental message of Deuteronomy is that there is one Lord, who is the God of Israel. He is a loving and caring God, and he demonstrated his power when he led the Israelites out of Egyptian bondage. The nations worshipped many gods, but the Lord God is unique and superior in every way. See Deut. 4:32-39.

- ❖ **Covenant Loyalty.** God chooses Israel to be his special people, and he desires their hearts and devotion. They are chosen, not because of their greatness, but because of God's lovingkindness, and they are to respond with covenant loyalty. See Deut. 7:6-11.

- ❖ **The Law.** The covenant law is repeated in Deuteronomy, including the foundational Ten Commandments (5:6-21). Moses instructs the people to put the words in their heart and obey it. Their love for God and obedience to the covenant are connected. See Deut. 7:12-16.

- ❖ **Instruction.** The covenant is to be passed down from generation to generation. Parents are to teach their children, instructing them of what God has done for them and teaching them to obey God's law. Children are to honor their parents and heed their instruction. See Deut. 4:9-14.

- ❖ **A Holy People.** Israel is a special people, a people of God's own possession. They are chosen to be a vessel for God's purposes. As they enter into a foreign land, the people are tasked with living a godly life and pointing others to their great God. They are equally warned not to be influenced by the nations and led into immorality and idolatry. See Deut. 26:16-19.

- ❖ **The Land.** Moses speaks to the people as they prepare to enter the land of Canaan. The laws of Deuteronomy are cast in light of living in the land, and they apply to the unique challenges that Israel will face in Canaan. Obedience to the law means that Israel will live well in the land and prosper. Disobedience will result in being removed from the land. See Deut. 5:33.

Lesson 2

Historical Review of the Covenant

Deuteronomy 1-3

History of the Covenant	Principles of the Covenant	Stipulations of the Covenant	Consequences of the Covenant	The Choice of the Covenant	Continuity of the Covenant
Deut. 1-4	Deut. 5-11	Deut. 12-26	Deut. 27-28	Deut. 29-30	Deut. 31-34
1st Speech	2nd Speech			3rd Speech	Epilogue

Historical Review (1:6-3:29)

The historical prologue was a common element of covenants, detailing the prior relationship between the two parties of the covenant. It often depicted the king's goodness and the vassal's dependence upon the king. The next section in Deuteronomy (1:6-3:29) contains a historical review of the life of Israel from their departure from Sinai to their arrival in Moab. The history is a first-person remembrance of events as told by Moses to the Israelites.

The History's Emphasis
1. God's Promise to Israel's Fathers.
2. God's Faithfulness to the Covenant.
3. Israel's Unfaithfulness to the Covenant.
4. Consequences of Covenant Obedience and Disobedience.

"See, I have set the land before you" (1:8a; also 1:21)

The opening verses of the history (1:6-8) recount God's instruction to leave Mt. Sinai and occupy the land of Canaan while situating the covenant within the promise that God gave to the nation's forefathers Abraham, Isaac, and Jacob. The prospect of life in the land dominates the book of Deuteronomy.

1. Why do you think the historical prologue begins with the covenant at Mt. Sinai instead of creation or the promises to Abraham?

Sweeter Than Honey Deuteronomy

The rest of the history focuses on six episodes within the life of Israel that reveal God's faithfulness and Israel's unfaithfulness to the covenant. The history in Deuteronomy mainly finds parallel accounts in Numbers with a brief episode in Exodus 18. The history is not a mere repetition, but it adds new insights and information that is not contained previously. While reading the historical review in Deuteronomy, focus on its purpose of showing God's goodness, Israel's dependence, and the consequences of obedience or disobedience.

The six episodes or groups of events can be coupled together through a chiastic structure with each pair showing a positive and a negative outcome.

- Episode 1 shows Moses relieved of the burden of leadership through the appointment of other judges and leaders whereas episode 6 relays Moses being relieved of his leadership because of his sin.

- Episode 2 tells of Israel's failure to acquire the land of Canaan while episode 5 shows the division of the land in the Transjordan as a preview of the nation's entry into Canaan.

- Episodes 3 & 4 recount Israel's journey to their present location through the nations of Edom, Moab and the Amorites. God forbids engagement with Edom and Moab, but Sihon and Og are defeated because of their stubborn defiance.

Event	Exodus/Numbers	Deuteronomy
1. The appointment of judges to assist Moses	Ex. 18; Num. 11	Deut. 1:9-18
2. The twelve spies and their aftermath	Num. 13-14	Deut. 1:19-46
3. Israel travels around Edom, through Moab	Num. 20-21	Deut. 2:1-25
4. Israel defeats Sihon and Og	Num. 21:21-35	Deut. 2:26-3:11
5. The division of the Transjordan land	Num. 32	Deut. 3:12-22
6. Moses requested and denied entry into Canaan	Num. 27:12-14	Deut. 3:23-29

Episode 1: Appointment of Judges (1:9-18)

The first story in Moses' history seems to combine two prior episodes in the life of Moses. When Moses meets with Jethro before he arrives at Mt. Sinai, his father-in-law suggests that he appoint judges to help him address the concerns of the people (Ex. 18:13-26). Right before Moses departs from Sinai, he cries out to God over the burden of the people's complaints (Num. 11:10-17).

2. Why have the people multiplied according to v. 9-11?

Lesson 2

3. Who is responsible for Moses' burden according to v. 12?

4. This portion of Israel's history doesn't seem to be the most prominent. Why is it chosen as the first account in Moses' history? Why is it an appropriate introduction to the covenant?

5. What kind of judgments does Moses command the people to make?

6. Identify the following elements (if any) within this section:

God's Goodness:	The People's Dependence:	Consequences:

Episode 2: The Twelve Spies (1:19-46)

The remainder of chapter 1 records the pivotal events at Kadesh when Israel listens to the faithless report of the twelve spies. This account includes four parts: the sending of the spies (1:19-25), the people's rebellion by listening to the faithless spies (1:26-33), the punishment of the rebellion (1:34-40), and Israel's failed attempt to take the land (1:41-46).

The Land
- Given to Israel (1:20)
- Set before them (1:21)
- Instructed to go up and take possession (1:21)

7. How is the wilderness described in 1:19?

Sweeter Than Honey Deuteronomy

8. Who makes the request for the spies to enter the land? See Deut. 1:22 and Num. 13:1-15.

9. Identify the following elements (if any) within this section:

God's Goodness:	The People's Dependence:	Consequences:

Episode 3 & 4: Encountering the Nations (2:1-3:11)

When Israel's wilderness wandering ends, the Lord directs the people along the eastern side of the land of Canaan. Along the way they encounter various nations, many of whom are relatives of Israel. The Lord helps Israel navigate their journey safely to their destination.

> **At Horeb**: "You have stayed long enough at this mountain" (1:6).
> ------------------------------------
> **In the Wilderness**: "You have been traveling around this mountain country long enough" (2:3)

10. Identify the following elements (if any) within this section:

God's Goodness:	The People's Dependence:	Consequences:

11. Identify God's instructions to Israel on their journey.

Nation	God's Instruction	Reason Given
Edom (2:1-8)		
Moab (2:9-15)		
Ammon (2:16-23)		
Sihon, king of Heshbon (2:24-37)		
Og, king of Bashan (3:1-11)		

Episode 5: Division of the Transjordan Land (3:12-22)

After defeating the nations in the Transjordan region, the land is granted to Reuben, Gad and Manasseh. These three tribes are still expected to cross over into Canaan and fight for possession of that land.

12. What does Moses require of the men of the Transjordan tribes?

13. What encouragement does Moses give to Joshua?

Sweeter Than Honey Deuteronomy

Episode 6: Moses' Request and Denial to Enter Canaan (3:23-29)

Moses pleads with the Lord one final time to enter the land, but his request is denied. Instead, he is granted the opportunity to see the land, and he is instructed to encourage Joshua in future leadership.

> On three occasions, Moses states that the Lord was angry with him "because of you" [Israelites] (1:37; 3:26; 4:21)

14. What provision does God give Moses?

15. What does God instruct Moses to do for Joshua?

16. What lessons do we learn from the punishment of Moses?

Lesson 3

The Foundation of the Covenant
Deuteronomy 4

History of the Covenant	Principles of the Covenant	Stipulations of the Covenant	Consequences of the Covenant	The Choice of the Covenant	Continuity of the Covenant
Deut. 1-4	Deut. 5-11	Deut. 12-26	Deut. 27-28	Deut. 29-30	Deut. 31-34
1st Speech	2nd Speech			3rd Speech	Epilogue

Sermon (ch. 4)

Deuteronomy 1-3 provide a chronological review of Israel's history from their time at Mt. Sinai to their present circumstances on the plains of Moab. Chapter 4 completes the first speech of Moses, and it continues to highlight some historical events, like the Exodus (4:20, 34, 37), the revelation at Mt. Sinai (4:9-14), and God's judgment at Baal of Peor (4:3). Deuteronomy 4 displays a change in tone and style, moving away from a strict historical review to a sermon, filled with exhortation and encouragement. Israel's history is not intended to be an academic exercise, but it is relayed to encourage obedience to God and the covenant. The past serves as a lesson for their present and future obedience. As such, this chapter gets at the very heart of Deuteronomy, establishing a foundation for the nation's identity as found in their covenant with God.

Deut. 1-3	Deut. 4
Historical Review	Sermon
Recollection	Exhortation
Past	Present & Future

Yahweh Alone is God

4:1-8	**There is No Other God** (reflection on 1st commandment)
4:9-31	**Do Not Make Idols** (reflection on 2nd commandment)
4:32-40	**There is No Other God** (reflection on 1st commandment)

The underlying theme of the sermon is that the Lord alone is God. It can be further divided into three sections, arranged in a basic chiasm or concentric structure.

The first section (4:1-8) and the final section (4:32-40) stress obedience to the Sovereign God of Israel. As such, it provides a reflection on the First Commandment of the covenant, that Israel should have no other gods. It includes positive commands to keep the law and do it (see 4:1-2, 40 for key verses in each section). The central section of the

Sweeter Than Honey Deuteronomy

sermon reflects upon the Second Commandment of the covenant, which forbids idolatry. It includes the warning to "take care" (4:9) and "watch yourselves very carefully" (4:15) in the new land and in the presence of the next generations. This sermon provides a fitting introduction to the Ten Commandments, which are recounted in chapter 5.

First Section (4:1-8)

The sermon begins with the transition, "And now," looking beyond what happened in the past to present needs and future life in the land. The people are called to "hear" and "do" the statutes and laws that Moses is teaching. The need for obedience is found in the opening words and establishes one of the main themes of the sermon. Two reasons for obedience are provided in this section.

> **Reason #1:** They are told to obey "that you may live" (v. 1). Obedience is the key to life. The people are reminded of God's judgment at Baal of Peor. Those that sinned against the Lord perished but those who held fast "are all alive today" (v 4).
>
> **Reason #2:** They are called to obey "for that will be your wisdom and your understanding in the sight of the peoples" (v. 6). Obedience will impact the nations around them for good. They will be elevated in the sight of the people because of the God they serve and the law they possess.

1. Moses commands the people not to add to or take away from the law. What does this say about the nature of the law?

2. What would the nations learn about Israel from their obedience?

3. Will obeying God today have a similar impact?

4. Does this section reveal a positive or negative view of the law?

Lesson 3

Second Section (4:9-31)

The middle section includes three subsections as Moses calls upon the people to remember the past revelation of God at Mt. Sinai (v. 9-14), guard their hearts against idolatry (v. 15-24), and remain steadfast in the land before their children (v. 25-31). Once again, this section highlights the use of past history to shape their hearts in the present and obedience in the future.

Moses calls upon the people to take care "lest you forget" what happened when God revealed himself at Mt. Sinai. The key message comes in v. 12:

> At Mt. Sinai, you heard my voice but saw no form (v. 9-14).
>
>
>
> Therefore, you shall not make an idol (v. 15-24).
>
>
>
> So that you may live long in the land (v. 24-31).

"You heard the sound of words but saw no form; there was only a voice."

The point is that God revealed himself through the spoken word and without a visible form. Their job was to obey his voice, not attempt to create an image out of physical objects.

God is...
Unseen (v. 12)
Jealous (v. 24)
Merciful (v. 31)
Unique (v. 35, 39)

One of the lessons to learn from Mt. Sinai is that they should not make any idols or carved images. Verses 15-24 contain clear prohibitions against idolatry in all its many forms. Instead, the people are to be a special people (v. 20), remember the covenant, and refrain from idolatry (v. 23-24).

Moses concludes the middle section by returning to the consequences of disobedience and obedience, namely death and life (v. 24-31). If they forsake the covenant and make an idol, they will perish in the land (v. 26). If they repent, however, they will be forgiven (v. 29-30).

5. How can God be both a "consuming fire, a jealous God" (v. 24) and a merciful God (v. 31)?

6. How do the prohibitions against idolatry in v. 16-19 relate to the elements of creation? Do you notice anything about the order in which they are listed in Deuteronomy?

Sweeter Than Honey Deuteronomy

7. When does Moses suggest that the people might fall into idolatry (v. 25)? What does this suggest about the temptations that come with the passing of time? How can they combat that?

8. What language does Moses use to describe the exodus in v. 20? Why do you think he chose to use that language?

9. The last section talked about the potential for influence if they obeyed. What would happen to the people in relation to the nations if they disobeyed?

Israel's unique experiences (v. 32-38).

The Lord is God; there is no other (v. 39).

Therefore, you shall keep the law (v. 40).

Third Section (4:32-40)

Israel's experience is unique in human history, spanning all time and geography (v. 32). Their unique experiences could only come from a unique God.

> *"Know therefore today, and lay it to your heart, that the LORD is God in heaven above and on the earth beneath; there is no other"* (v. 39).

The knowledge of God should yield obedience (v. 40). Moses again emphasizes the consequence of obedience, which would yield life and wellness for the people in the land.

10. What unique experiences does Moses identify?

v. 33, 36

v. 34, 37

11. Does v. 38 refer to what God has already done or what God will accomplish?

12. What was the goal of the exodus according to v. 35? What role would this play in their covenant with God?

Narrative Conclusion (4:41-49)

Chapter 4 ends with a narrative conclusion in two parts. First, Moses sets aside three cities on the eastern side of the Jordan as cities of refuge (v. 41-43). Second, the concluding statement indicates the conclusion of Moses' first speech (v. 44-49). This concluding statement finishes where the speech starts, with a summary of Israel's location in Moab and defeat of the Amorite kings Sihon and Og.

"This is the law that Moses set before the people of Israel" (v. 44).

Sweeter Than Honey Deuteronomy

Lesson 4

The Ten Commandments
Deuteronomy 5

History of the Covenant	Principles of the Covenant	Stipulations of the Covenant	Consequences of the Covenant	The Choice of the Covenant	Continuity of the Covenant
Deut. 1-4	**Deut. 5-11**	Deut. 12-26	Deut. 27-28	Deut. 29-30	Deut. 31-34
1st Speech	\multicolumn{3}{c}{2nd Speech}	3rd Speech	Epilogue

God Talks to the People at Mt. Sinai (5:1-5)

"Hear, O Israel, the statutes and the rules that I speak in your hearing today, and you shall learn them and be careful to do them" (5:1).

Moses calls upon Israel to hear the law, consisting of statutes and rules. Having heard it, they are called to learn and obey them. Moses then recalls the Lord's revelation at Mt. Sinai.

1. Who does God make the covenant with according to v. 2-3?

The Ten Commandments (5:6-21)

The Ten Commandments, called the "Ten Words" in the text (Ex. 34:28; Deut. 10:4), form the foundation of God's covenant law with Israel. This set of commandments stands as a special and unique portion of the law for several reasons:

- **Primary Position.** The Ten Commandments are the first laws given and possess a primary position related to the rest of the covenant law. Based upon their position and unique content, they provide an appropriate introduction to the rest of the law.
- **Direct Communication.** The Ten Commandments are spoken directly by God to the people (Deut. 5:4-5). The rest of the law will be mediated through Moses at the request of the people.

- **Distinct Form.** The Ten Commandments are given in the form of general instructions (apodictic laws). In contrast, the other law generally takes the form of case law, which involves regulations of particular situations.

> **Two Types of Laws**
>
> **Casuistic Laws** or case laws are laws based upon conditional events. They take the form, "If..." you do this, "then..." this should happen. The *if* clause is called the protasis and the *then* clause is called the apodosis.
>
> **Apodictic Laws** consist of absolute but general principles. They state the ideal behavior without taking into consideration mitigating circumstances. They take the form, "You shall [not] ..."

- **Foundational Content.** The commandments can be divided into two parts. The first part (Commands 1-4) relates to Israel's relationship with God and establish the necessary loyalty and devotion they should have toward him. The second part (Commands 5-10) relate to Israel's relationship with one another. These commands cover matters important to nearly all other law codes, protecting the family relationship, the sanctity of life, property rights and justice in the court system.
- **Summary Function.** Based upon their unique position and overarching principles, the Ten Commandments serve as an appropriate summary and interpretive key for the rest of the law. Jesus argues that the most important laws are loving God and loving neighbor (Matt. 22:37-40), upon which all the Law and the Prophets depend, and the Ten Commandments summarize.

#1 *You shall have no other gods before me* **(5:6-7).** Verse 6 serves as a prologue, but it leads into the First Commandment and elaborates on who God is. He is the God of the Exodus, the one who brought the people out of the land of Egypt, out of the house of slavery. It is this God who must have priority. God has no rival, and no other gods should come before him. He is the only Sovereign and true God, and He must be recognized as such. The First Commandment is foundational in the covenant, the book of Deuteronomy, the history of Israel contained in the Old Testament, and all of the Bible.

2. Why would other gods take a priority over God? What motivation would people have for turning to other gods?

Lesson 4

#2 ***You shall not make for yourself a carved image* (5:8-10).** God prohibits the making of any carved image or physical likeness. Carved images receive "worship" and "service" (v 9), rivaling what should be given to God. The word for likeness is the same word found in 4:15 where it states that God's "form" or likeness was not seen at Mt. Sinai. God has never been seen by man, and his image cannot be captured by human hands. God is living and powerful as opposed to idols, which are lifeless, mute, and powerless. An idol would not capture the essence of God but simply diminish it.

3. What types of likenesses are forbidden in v. 8?

4. Does this command prohibit creating an idol of Yahweh, the other gods, or both?

5. What reason does God give for not worshipping idols in v. 9?

#3 ***You shall not take the Lord's name in vain* (5:11).** This command can be literally rendered, "You shall not lift up the name of the Lord your God to vanity." The name is representative of the person, and so, forbids trivialization of God himself. The command has commonly been applied to blasphemy or minimizing God's name in speech, but that understanding may be too limiting in the scope of what's involved in this command. It could involve anything that would bring dishonor or dismiss God's character of greatness. Other possibilities for lifting God's name in vain could refer to corrupt worship or dishonest oaths in the Lord's name, particularly in a court case (Isa. 48:1; Jer. 4:1).

6. Are there other ways that God's name could be lifted up to vanity?

7. How does this command primarily address our attitude, and how does it relate to the previous commands?

#4 **Observe the Sabbath day (5:12-15).** The 4th Command has more space devoted to it than any other, comprising 4 verses. These verses provide the command (v. 12), the definition of observance (v. 13), the rationale (v. 14a), the scope (v. 14b) and the motivation for observance (v. 15). The Sabbath day is to be "observed" and kept "holy," which involves, but may not be limited to, resting from labor. The Sabbath belongs to the Lord; time and rest are gifts from the Lord and should be freely acknowledged as coming from him. The motivation for the command is rooted in the Exodus, where God delivered the people from slavery.

8. How does this command relate to the previous commands? Do they help define what it means to observe the Sabbath? If so, how?

9. Does Sabbath observance include more than resting from labor? What else might be involved to "keep it holy"?

10. Who is included in the Sabbath observance?

11. How does the motivation in Deuteronomy differ from Exodus? (see Ex. 20:11 and Deut. 5:15). Why might this change be made?

Lesson 4

#5 ***Honor your father and your mother* (5:16).** The 5th command begins the group of laws related to a person's responsibility to his neighbor. By addressing the family relationship, the cornerstone of society, it bears a place of prominence. The command charges children (and adults) to honor and respect their parents. The negative counterpart of this commandment involves dishonoring or cursing, and it incurs the death penalty (Ex. 21:17; Deut. 27:16). The consequence of this command is long life in the land, which corresponds with the final verse of Moses' sermon and relates to continuing the covenant into future generations (4:40). Parents are instructed to teach their children (4:9-10). For the teaching to take root, children must listen to their parents and honor their instruction.

12. What kind of things are involved in honoring father and mother?

13. How should a child treat a parent who does not act honorably?

#6 ***You shall not murder* (5:17).** The main word in this passage means "to kill, murder, strike down, slay" (HALOT). It refers to the intentional murder of another individual, but the word also incorporates unintentional killing or manslaughter (the same word is used in Num. 35:6 to refer to manslaughter). All humans possess a sanctity of life derived from being made in the image of God (Gen. 9:6). Murder is a violation of this dignity and right to life that every person possesses. The command does not prohibit capital punishment (Deut. 17:2-7; 19:12) or killing in war (Deut. 20-21), which are regulated elsewhere.

14. How does murder differ from capital punishment of killing in warfare?

15. Does the principle behind this command extend beyond the prohibition to murder? If so, how?

#7 ***You shall not commit adultery*** **(5:18).** Adultery, defined as the sexual relationship between a married person and someone other than their spouse, is strictly forbidden. Marriage is a sacred institution, ordained by God. In marriage, a man and a woman are joined together in a lifelong, committed relationship. Other sexual sins are harmful and addressed elsewhere in the law (Num. 25:1; Deut. 22:21; 23:17-18), but adultery is particularly detrimental because it involved the breaking of a covenant commitment between a husband and wife. For this reason, adultery serves as an image for Israel's idolatry and unfaithfulness toward God (see Hos. 1-2; Ezek. 16).

16. In adultery, who does a person sin against?

17. What are the consequences of adultery? Consider all those who could be affected.

#8 ***You shall not steal*** **(5:19).** The 8th commandment protects property rights and prohibits taking that which belongs to another. The law is a general prohibition and includes the theft of anything that belongs to another. The word for theft in this law is also used in reference to kidnapping, whether for the purpose of slavery or profit (Ex 21:16; Deut. 24:7). An example of this kind of theft can be seen in the treatment of Joseph by his brothers (Ex. 37:18-28).

18. Does the inclusion of kidnapping within this command extend your understanding of the law? Does this further shape the principle behind the law?

Lesson 4

#9 ***You shall not bear false witness against your neighbor* (5:20).** The verse can be literally rendered, "You shall not respond with worthless testimony." The instruction includes the need for honesty in general, but it extends to telling the truth in testimony, which would most likely be given in a court of law. As such, it calls for justice and truthfulness in the court as a protection for every citizen. "Worthless" testimony is often directed against the weak and helpless and associated with a complete abandonment of the law (see Ex. 23:1-3; Lev. 19:15-16; Deut. 19:16-21; Amos 5:12-13).

19. Why might someone bear false witness against his neighbor?

20. What does a society look like that disregards justice in the court system?

#10 ***You shall not covet* (5:21).** The last command prohibits coveting and inappropriate desires or cravings. As the final command, it provides a filter through which to understand all the previous commands. The law often regulates outward actions, but God has always been concerned with the heart as the foundation of obedience and devotion to God. The heart and actions are connected; to love God is to keep the commandments.

21. What is a person prohibited from coveting in this passage?

22. Does this command relate to any of the other Ten Commandments? If so, how?

Sweeter Than Honey Deuteronomy

Israel's Response at Mt. Sinai (5:22-33)

Moses reminds the people of their terror when they heard God speak from Mt. Sinai. They pleaded with Moses to resume his role as mediator and retrieve the rest of the law for them. God listened to their request and did not speak directly to them anymore. God then spoke the law to Moses, impressing upon him the need for obedience and the consequences it would bring.

23. Why do the people say they need a mediator?

24. Are the people commended or condemned for their request for a mediator?

25. How does God describe the type of obedience needed?

26. Underline the three consequences of obedience in the passage below.

> You shall walk in all the way that the Lord your God has commanded you, that you may live, and that it may go well with you, and that you may live long in the land that you shall possess (Deut. 5:33).

Lesson 5

Election and Testing

Deuteronomy 6-7

History of the Covenant	**Principles of the Covenant**	Stipulations of the Covenant	Consequences of the Covenant	The Choice of the Covenant	Continuity of the Covenant
Deut. 1-4	**Deut. 5-11**	Deut. 12-26	Deut. 27-28	Deut. 29-30	Deut. 31-34
1st Speech	\multicolumn{3}{c}{2nd Speech}	3rd Speech	Epilogue

| 1st Speech | 2nd Speech | | | 3rd Speech | Epilogue |

That You May Live Long in the Land (6:1-3)

After God spoke the 10 Commandments to all the people of Israel, he instructs Moses privately regarding the "whole commandment and the statutes and the rules" (5:31). Deuteronomy 6:1-3 states that "now this" is the commandment that Moses received, the same one that he is telling the next generation.

Good life and prosperity in the Promised Land depend upon the people's obedience and keeping the covenant. The reward of covenant faithfulness is made several times in close proximity as Moses instructs the people on the importance of obedience and teaching the next generation (4:40; 5:16; 5:32-33; 6:1-3, 18).

Teaching the Next Generation (6:4-25)

Sustained success in the Promised Land will depend upon Israel's ability to teach and instruct the next generation. In Deuteronomy 6 Moses continues to shape Israel's identity through their past experiences of God's gracious activity and their future adherence to the covenant. Covenant faithfulness requires taking seriously the law in their own lives, learning from past mistakes, and intentionally teaching their children to know God. Chapter 6 contains two warnings for the future generation, sandwiched in between positive instructions to teach your children.

> **Structure of Deut. 6:4-25**
>
> Teach your children (6:4-9)
>   Do not forget the Lord (6:10-15)
>   Do not test the Lord (6:16-19)
> Teach your children (6:20-25)

Sweeter Than Honey Deuteronomy

The Sh'ma (6:4-9)

This section begins with a foundational summary statement of *what* is to be believed, practiced, and taught to the next generation. It encompasses the heart of the covenant by relaying God's essential nature and the fitting response to such a God. God is singular in nature, and he requires a singular devotion

> Hear, O Israel:
> The LORD our God, the Lord is one.
> You shall love the Lord your God
>   with all your heart
>   and with all your soul
>   and with all your might
>   (Deut. 6:4-5)

from his people, characterized by love. Love is a fundamental part of the covenant, and it suggests that the relationship between God and man is more than just keeping a list of rules and laws. It is a devotion that springs from the heart and the entire being, resulting in honor, loyalty, and obedience. Jesus cites this instruction to love God as the single greatest commandment and a summary of the law (Matt. 22:34-40).

> **Sh'ma Yisrael.** "Hear O, Israel" serve as the opening words for one of the most important and foundational statements in the Scripture. There is one God and he requires complete devotion (Deut. 6:4-5). Today, Jews use the designation, "Sh'ma Yirsael" to refer to a collection of daily readings and prayers, which consist of Deut. 6:4-9; 11:13-21 and Num. 15:37-41. Jews are encouraged to recite the Sh'ma as a standard statement of their faith.

1. What does it mean that "the LORD is one"?

2. How does the sh'ma relate to the first two of the 10 Commandments?

3. What kind of love is required for God? How does this differ from the world's view of love?

Lesson 5

Three Ways of Teaching

| 1. With Frequent Conversation (6:7-9) | 2. By Reciting God's Past Actions (6:20-23) | 3. By Encouraging Obedience to God's Laws (6:24-25) |

Teaching Children (6:4-25)

In this chapter, Moses elaborates on the type of teaching that should come from Israelite parents. Parents should engage in a steady stream of teaching, both in regular, daily conversation and reminders of the law in the home (6:7-9). Opportunity to teach can come from questions posed by children (6:20-25). Regular, religious practices will naturally prompt questions about their purpose and meaning. These questions can be answered by placing the covenant in the context of what God has done for his people by releasing them from Egyptian bondage and bringing to the land. The law is a component of liberty and enjoying a good life in the land.

4. When should Israelite parents teach their children?

5. What does it mean to bind the law "as a sign on your hand" and "frontlets between your eyes"?

6. How should Israelite parents talk about the law? What are the benefits of obedience?

7. Should a child be given an explanation or reason for obedience?

Sweeter Than Honey Deuteronomy

Warnings (6:10-19)

Sandwiched between the instructions on teaching are two warnings.

> God is identified as a **Jealous God** three times in three chapters (4:24; 5:9; 6:15).

Warning #1: Do not forget the Lord **(6:10-15)**. As Israel enjoyed blessings in the land, they would be tempted to forget the Lord and pursue the idolatry of their neighbors in the land.

Warning #2: Do not test the Lord **(6:16-19)**. In times of trials, Israel will be tempted to grumble against God and doubt his ability to provide like they did at Massah (Ex. 17:2-7).

8. How does Moses describe the condition in the land when they may be tempted to forget the Lord?

9. What does Israel need to do to avoid repeating the sin at Massah?

A Holy People (ch. 7)

Deuteronomy 7 continues the discussion from the previous chapter, combining the faithfulness of the next generation with warnings of potential dangers. The main instruction comes first (v. 1-5), which is then followed by reasons for obedience grounded in God's character (v. 6-10). Then, Moses talks about God's provision for Israel in the land, both in terms of blessings in the land (v. 11-16) and the defeat of Israel's enemies (v. 17-24). Having destroyed the people, they must then destroy their idols (v. 25-26).

> **Structure of Deut. 7**
>
> *Main Instruction*: Destroy the Nations and Be Separate (v. 1-5)
> *God's Character*: Gracious and Faithful (v. 6-10)
> *God's Provision*: Good Life in the Land and the Defeat of Enemies (v. 11-24)
> *Second Instruction*: Destroy the Idols in the Land (v. 25-26)

The key point of this passage is to remain separate in the land. Moses provides four instructions to ensure their distinctiveness as a people.

> **Instructions for Being a Separate People**
>
> 1. You must devote the nations to complete destruction (v. 2a).
> 2. You shall make no covenant with them (v. 2b).
> 3. You shall not intermarry with them (v. 3-4).
> 4. You shall not covet their idols but destroy them (v. 5, also v. 25-26).

Lesson 5

"For you are a people holy to the LORD your God" (v. 6). Having established their need for holiness, Moses roots Israel's identity in the distinct nature and character of God, specifying two reasons that Israel should be a holy and distinct people. Moses concludes by instructing strict obedience to the covenant law (v. 11).

> ***Reason #1: God's Choice* (7:6-8).** Israel's distinct nature stems from God's choice. God chose Israel, not because of their superiority, but because of God's grace and love.
>
> ***Reason #2: God's Faithfulness* (7:9-10).** God is a faithful God and he will not turn away from those who love him. He cannot, however, overlook sin, and he will bring judgment upon the wicked.

Israel's success would be dependent upon their great God. If they respond to him with obedience, he will provide for the people's needs.

> ***God's Provision #1: Blessings in the Land* (7:12-16).** If Israel remains faithful to the covenant through their obedience, God will remain faithful and bless the people in the land.
>
> ***God's Provision #2: Victory Over their Enemies* (7:17-24).** Israel will be tempted to fear the stronger and mightier nations around them, but they need only trust in the Lord. God will provide victory for them and allow them to completely destroy the Canaanite nations.

10. When would Israel be tempted to forget the Lord?

11. What steps does Israel need to take to remain a distinct people?

12. What kinds of things do Christians need to do today to remain distinct?

13. Why did God choose Israel? Are we any different today? How should God's choice affect the attitude of God's people?

14. What blessings would God grant for Israel in the new land?

15. How would idols be alluring to Israel?

16. Why might Israel be afraid to possess the land? What should they consider when they are afraid?

Lesson 6

Remember and Do Not Forget

Deuteronomy 8-9

History of the Covenant	Principles **of the** **Covenant**	Stipulations of the Covenant	Consequences of the Covenant	The Choice of the Covenant	Continuity of the Covenant
Deut. 1-4	**Deut. 5-11**	Deut. 12-26	Deut. 27-28	Deut. 29-30	Deut. 31-34
1st Speech	\multicolumn{3}{c}{2nd **Speech**}			3rd Speech	Epilogue

A Call to Remember (ch. 8-9)

Having instructed the Israelites on their need to be a distinct people, Moses proceeds to shape a distinct attitude. The people already possess the key components for developing a godly attitude, needing only to look to their prior relationship with God. For this reason, Moses calls upon the people to learn from their past. Four times the people are told to remember (8:2, 18; 9:7, 27) and four additional times they are told not to forget (8:11, 14, 19; 9:7).

God intends to bring the people into the Promised Land, providing victory over the inhabitants and providing them with the bounty of the land. These future successes and blessings will provide a potential temptation for arrogance and self-reliance.

1. Identify the potential threat to Israel's attitude below.

	8:17-18	9:4-5
Israel's Circumstances		
Israel's Potential Boast		
Real Reason for Israel's Circumstances		

2. Moses uses Israel's past experience to combat these potential faulty claims. Identify the specific events he calls to Israel's remembrance below.

Lessons from the Past	8:2	9:7

Humility and Pride (8:1-20)

The conclusion of the argument from Deuteronomy 8 can be found in verses 17-18. God is the reason that they could enjoy the blessing of the land, not their own might. To make this point, Moses alternates between two opposing images throughout the chapter:

> **1) The Wilderness, Scarcity, and Humility**
>
> **2) The Land, Fullness and Pride**

3. Complete the next page before answering the next two questions.

4. Is this only a problem for Israel? What can Christians today learn today from this chapter?

5. On what occasion is Deuteronomy 8:3 quoted in the New Testament? What point is being made there?

Lesson 6

Wilderness, Scarcity, & Humility

God's Testing (8:1-5)

Exhortation (v. 1)

a. What are the consequences of obedience?

b. How does God test Israel? Why?

God's Testing (8:15-16)

f. How is God described?

g. Why does God humble and test the people?

Consequences (8:19-20)

i. What will happen to the people if they forget the Lord?

The Land, Fullness, and Pride

God's Intentions (8:6-10)

Exhortation (v. 6)

c. How is the land described?

Potential Threat (8:11-14)

Exhortation (v. 11)

d. How will Israel "live" and "multiply" (v. 1) in the land?

e. What does Moses warn against in their prosperity?

Summary Instruction (8:17-18)

Exhortation (v. 17)

h. What is the connection between disobedience and the heart/mind?

Sweeter Than Honey Deuteronomy

A Consuming Fire (9:1-29)

Deuteronomy 9 builds upon the argument of the previous chapter. It is not because of Israel's might that they will enjoy the land. In fact, they are going to dispossess "greater and mightier" nations (9:1). Israel will gain the land because God is greater than any nation, and he will conquer the inhabitants and

"Know therefore today that he who goes over before you as **A CONSUMING FIRE** is the Lord your God" (Deut. 9:3).

give the land to Israel. God is a consuming fire and he will wipe away the nations before them.

6. How does Moses describe the strength and might of the inhabitants of Canaan?

Israel might be tempted to conclude that their righteousness led God to give them the land. Again, Moses wants Israel to look into their past to learn some lessons. Israel is not righteous or morally superior, but they are a stubborn and rebellious people. Moses argues that Israel has continually been rebellious, from Egypt until today. This section identifies the ways that Israel had sinned before God, and it is framed by two statements of their continual disobedience (9:6-7, 24).

7. In the boxes below, identify the places and sins that Moses calls to memory for Israel.

Israel provoked the Lord to wrath from *"Egypt until you came to this place"* (9:6-8)		
9:8-21	9:22	9:23

"You have been rebellious against the Lord from the day that I knew you" (9:24)

8. What images of fire are found in the text? See Deut. 9:3, 10, 15, 21.

Lesson 6

Moses spends a great deal of time on God's desire to destroy the people and his intercessory prayer. He returns to these events after summarizing Israel's continual sin (9:18-21, 25-29).

9. Identify the arguments that Moses makes to God to forgive the people.

Argument #1 (v. 26)	
Argument #2 (v. 27)	
Argument #3 (v. 28)	

Sweeter Than Honey Deuteronomy

Lesson 7

Humble and Devoted Hearts
Deuteronomy 10-11

History of the Covenant	**Principles of the Covenant**	Stipulations of the Covenant	Consequences of the Covenant	The Choice of the Covenant	Continuity of the Covenant
Deut. 1-4	**Deut. 5-11**	Deut. 12-26	Deut. 27-28	Deut. 29-30	Deut. 31-34
1st Speech	2nd Speech			3rd Speech	Epilogue

New Tablets of Stone (10:1-11)

In Deuteronomy 10, Moses addresses the rest of the story at Mt. Sinai (10:1-11) and Israel's responsibility in light of God's goodness before them (10:12-22).

Moses impresses on Israel their sinfulness and God's gracious kindness toward them.

History at Sinai (Deut. 9-10)
- The Covenant at Sinai (9:6-12)
- Israel's Sin at Sinai (9:7-21)
- Moses' Intercession (9:25-29)
- New Tablets of Stone (10:1-11)
- Israel's Response (10:12-22)

After the people sin at Mt. Sinai and Moses breaks the law tablets, God provides another set of tablets to be housed in the Ark of the Covenant. He allows the people to continue their journey to Canaan, which brings them to their current location.

1. In Exodus, the instructions for the construction of the Ark (Ex. 35:30-36:1; 37:1-9) come after the tablets are broken in Exodus 32-34? Who makes the Ark?

2. When is the Ark made according to Deuteronomy 10:1-5? Who makes it?

3. How might these differences be reconciled?

Sweeter Than Honey Deuteronomy

4. Why does Moses relay the creation of the new tablets of stone? What purpose would it have served within his overall point?

What Does the Lord Require of You? (10:12-22)

Moses next turns his attention to the implications for Israel. What happened in the past should shape Israel's identity and present reality. They should have developed character in their trials that would help them choose the right course of action.

5. Identify what the Lord requires according to Deut. 10:12-13.

   a)

   b)

   c)

   d)

   e)

6. Are these requirements for Israel's good or harm?

> And now, Israel, what does the LORD your God require of you, but to fear the LORD your God, to walk in all his ways, to love him, to serve the LORD your God with all your heart and with all your soul, and to keep the commandments and statutes of the LORD, which I am commanding you today for your good?
> (Deut. 10:12-13)

"Circumcise therefore the foreskin of your heart, and be no longer stubborn" (Deut. 10:16)

God made the covenant with Israel at Mt. Sinai as a fulfillment of the promise to Abraham, Isaac and Jacob. When God made a covenant with Abraham, he commanded circumcision as a physical sign of the covenant promise (See Genesis 17). However, God never merely wanted a physical marking. He wanted circumcision to be a pointer to the covenant relationship he shared with his people. So, Moses calls on Israel to circumcise their hearts.

7. What does it mean to circumcise the heart?

8. How does this action contrast with being "stubborn"?

9. How is God described in Deut. 10:17-18?

10. How should God's character shape Israel's actions?

A Call to Covenant Loyalty (11:1-32)

Deuteronomy 11 concludes the section on the principles of the covenant (Deut. 6-11) and will lead into the actual giving of the Law in chapters 12-26. This chapter can be divided into the following sections, arranged in chiasm, or an inverted symmetrical pattern. The outside sections call upon Israel to consider the past and future blessings and discipline of the Lord (11:1-7, 26-32). The next inner sections continue to consider the consequences of obedience, showing that dispossessing the nations and living well in the land are dependent upon Israel's covenant loyalty (11:8-17, 22-25). The central element of these verses is found in Deut. 11:18-21, and they command covenant faithfulness and parallel the Sh'ma, found in Deut. 6:4-9. The quotations from the Sh'ma serve to frame the entire section on the covenant principles (Deut. 6-11) with covenant loyalty serving as the major theme throughout.

A. Consider the past blessings and discipline of the Lord (11:1-7)
   B. Living well in the land dependent upon Israel's covenant loyalty (11:8-17)
      C. Lay these words on your heart (11:18-21)
   B'. Dispossessing the nations dependent upon Israel's covenant loyalty (11:22-25)
A'. Consider the future discipline and blessings of the Lord (11:26-32)

The Blessings and Discipline of the Lord (11:1-7, 26-32)

Moses first calls upon the people to consider the discipline of the Lord they witnessed in the past (11:1-7) before moving on to the future (11:26-32).

Sweeter Than Honey Deuteronomy

11. What examples of the Lord's discipline does Moses call to memory?

v. 3 _____

v. 4 _____

v. 5 _____

v. 6 _____

12. Should discipline only be equated with punishment? What else is involved in discipline?

13. Why would the word "discipline" be used with these examples?

"See, I am setting before you today a blessing and a curse" (11:26).

To conclude the chapter, Moses looks to the blessings and curses embedded within the covenant (11:26-32). These consequences will depend upon Israel's obedience or disobedience to the covenant. The blessings and curses mentioned here will be given in greater detail in Deut. 27-28.

14. On what mountain are the blessings to be set? The curses?

Dispossessing the Nations and Living Well in the Land (11:8-17, 22-25)

Moses extends the discussion of the consequences of obedience to two specific and immediate examples: living well in the land (11:8-17) and dispossessing the inhabitants of the land (11:22-25).

15. How does Canaan differ from Egypt? What would this mean for Israel?

16. What will happen if Israel's heart is deceived?

17. How much of the land will God give Israel?

Echoes of the Sh'ma		
Love God with all your heart, soul and might	6:5	11:13
These words shall be on your heart	6:6	11:18
Teach when you sit and walk, rise and lie down	6:7	11:19
Bind them as sign on hand, frontlets between eyes	6:8	11:18
Write them on doorposts of house and gates	6:9	11:20

Lay These Words on Your Heart (11:18-21)

The chiastic structure places an emphasis on the innermost section of the chapter (11:18-21). Moses returns to the fundamental instruction of the Sh'ma in Deut. 6:4-9. Love the Lord with your whole heart and teach your children to love God to the same degree. This is vital if the covenant is to continue to the next generation.

18. Where should Israel place "these words of mine" according to v. 18? What is involved in this?

19. Are there any differences between Deut. 6:4-9 and 11:18-21?

20. How long will God's promise stand?

Sweeter Than Honey Deuteronomy

Lesson 8

The Covenant Laws, Part 1

Deuteronomy 12-26

History of the Covenant	Principles of the Covenant	**Stipulations of the Covenant**	Consequences of the Covenant	The Choice of the Covenant	Continuity of the Covenant
Deut. 1-4	Deut. 5-11	**Deut. 12-26**	Deut. 27-28	Deut. 29-30	Deut. 31-34
1st Speech	\multicolumn{3}{c}{**2nd Speech**}		3rd Speech	Epilogue

Framing the Covenant Laws

"These are the statutes and rules that you shall be careful to do in the land that the Lord, the God of your fathers, has given you to possess, all the days that you live on the earth" (12:1).

Deuteronomy 12-26 continues the second speech, providing the laws of the covenant. The opening verse, beginning with "These are the statutes and the rules" accomplish the following:

- A transition from the previous section, repeating God's gift, the possession of the land, and a command to keep the statutes and rules (11:31-32; 12:1).

- A superscription that indicates a new section of material (as in 1:1; 4:44-45; 6:1; 29:1; 33:1).

- A bracket with the conclusion of this section that encourages obedience (26:16-19).

The legal material of Deut. 12-26 serves as the core of the book. The 10 Commandments and general principles of loyalty and obedience (Deut. 5-11) introduce the more specific elements found here. It is also framed by blessings and curses, both in the present context of renewal (11:26-28; 28:1-29:1) and future settlement in the land (11:29-32; 27:1-26). The structure emphasizes the choice that lies before Israel to obey or disobey the covenant.

> **The Laws and Their Consequences**
>
> A. Present Blessings and Curses (11:26-28)
>   B. Future Blessings and Curses (11:29-32)
>   C. The Covenant Stipulations (12:1-26:19)
>   B'. Future Blessings and Curses (27:1-26)
> A'. Present Blessings and Curses (28:1-29:1)
>
> - See Craigie, Deuteronomy (NICOT), p. 212

The laws cover many aspects of Israelite life including family instructions, religious observance, ceremonial purity, civil matters, criminal cases, and military preparations. One possible outline of laws can be seen below.

The Covenant Stipulations in Deuteronomy

I. Worship and Holiness (12:2-16:17)
- A. Centralized Worship (12:2-32)
- B. False Prophets and Bad Influences (13:1-18)
- C. Clean & Unclean Animals (14:1-21)
- D. Offerings to God & the Poor (14:22-15:23)
- E. The Three Annual Festivals (16:1-17)

II. Israel's Leaders (16:18-18:22)
- A. Judges and the Court (16:18-17:13)
- B. Kings (17:14-20)
- C. Priests and Levites (18:1-8)
- D. Prophets (18:9-22)

III. Criminal and Military Justice (19:1-22:8)
- A. Manslaughter & Witnesses (19:1-21)
- B. Warfare (20:1-20)
- C. Atonement for Unsolved Murder (21:1-9)
- D. Wives and Children (21:10-23)
- E. Preservation of Life (22:1-8)

IV. Purity (22:9-23:18)
- A. Unlawful Mixtures (22:9-12)
- B. Marriage (22:13-30)
- C. Exclusion from Assembly (23:1-18)

V. Interpersonal Affairs (23:19-25:19)
- A. Possessions of Others (23:19-24:7)
- B. Dignity of Others (24:8-25:4)
- C. Continued Progeny (25:5-12)
- D. Economic Justice & Amalekite Sin (25:13-19)

VI. Covenant Remembrance (26:1-15)
- A. Firstfruit Offerings (26:1-11)
- B. Third Year Tithe (26:12-15)

Arrangement of the Laws

The laws are loosely arranged by topic, but several possibilities have been suggested for how this arrangement unfolds. One possibility considers the top-down authority structures of the theocracy (a system of government where God and his laws function as the chief authority). The laws naturally begin (and end) with God and then proceed to the various agents for carrying out his will (see Block, Deuteronomy, NIVAC, p 301-302). Some students of Deuteronomy have noted a connection between the Ten Commandments and the ordering of the covenant stipulations. The ordering is not exact and contains gaps.

Responsibilities in Israelite Society
- Yahweh (12:2-16:17)
- Offices (16:18-21:9)
- Family (21:10-22:30)
- Community (23:1-8)
- Israelite Life (23:9-25:19)
- Worship (26:1-15)

Ten Commandments	Laws	Notes
#1-3 (Reverence God)	Deut. 12-13	Laws related to purity in worship
#4 (Keep Sabbath)	Deut. 14:28-16:17	Laws related to observance of days
#5 (Honor parents)	Deut. 16:18-18:22	Laws related to authority figures
#6 (Against Murder)	Deut. 19:1-21:9	Laws related to murder, manslaughter, and war
#7 (Against Adultery)	Deut. 22:13-30	Laws related to sexual conduct
#8 (Against Theft)	Deut. 23:19-24:7	Laws related to theft and kidnapping
#9 (About Witnesses)	Deut. 24:8-25:4	Laws related to justice
#10 (Against Coveting)	Deut. 25:5-16	Laws related to levirate marriage and honesty

Individual laws may be related to one another through other key words or concepts and not fit within the topical grouping. Yet, it appears that the Ten Commandments likely served some basis for ordering the laws.

The only consensus of the arrangement appears to be that the material begins and ends with laws related to God and worship with laws about responsibilities to others in between.

| Laws Related to God and Worship (12:1-16:17) | Laws Related to Others (16:18-25:19) | Laws Related to God and Worship (26:1-15) |

The Content of the Covenant Laws (ch. 12-26)

The covenant stipulations are many and varied, covering a large range of topics. The laws cover religious, civil and moral aspects of Israel life. Many of the same themes as holiness, being distinct, and refraining from idolatry are addressed in practical and specific detail. Below are summary statements and notes on each section.

Worship and Holiness (12:2-16:17)

In keeping with the theme in Deuteronomy, God receives the priority when it comes to the covenant stipulations. The opening section contains a series of laws related to worship and religious matters.

Chapter 12 sets the tone with a strong contrast between false worship and true worship. They are to destroy the "places where the nations… served their gods" (v 2) "but you shall seek the place that the Lord your God will choose… to put his name and make his habitation there" (v 5). The reference to the place of the Lord's choosing frames the section (12:5; 16:16) and can be found 18 times in these chapters.

Chapter 13 warns against harmful influences by issuing the death penalty against false prophets (v. 1-5), relatives or friends (v. 6-11) or even an entire city (v. 12-18) if they promote or openly practice idolatry.

Deut. 14:3-21 provides dietary laws with the opening prohibition, *"You shall not eat any abomination"* (14:3). The laws address allowances and prohibitions from land animals (v. 3-8), fish (v. 9-10), birds (v. 11-18) and insects (v. 19-20).

Laws in Deut. 12:2-16:17
- Centralized Worship (12:2-28)
- Avoiding the Influence of Idolatry (12:29-13:18)
- Cutting forbidden (14:1-2)
- Dietary Laws (14:3-21)
- Tithes (14:22-28)
- Release of Debt (15:1-11)
- Release of Slaves (15:12-18)
- Offering of Firstborn (15:19-23)
- Passover Feast (16:1-8)
- Feast of Weeks (16:9-12)
- Feast of Booths (16:13-15)
- Summary Feast Instruction (16:16-17)
- Appointment of Judges (16:18-20)
- Idolatry (16:21-22)

Sweeter Than Honey Deuteronomy

The latter portion of chapter 14 begins a larger section of laws related to regular observances in the Israelite calendar, and it includes the following items:

- Giving of the tithe (14:22-29) year by year (14:22) and every three years (14:28)
- Release of debts (15:1-11) to be conducted every seven years (15:1)
- Release of slaves (15:12-18) to occur in the seventh year (15:12)
- Giving of firstlings (15:19-23) to be occur each year (15:20)
- Annual feasts of Passover (16:1-7), Weeks (16:9-12) and Booths (16:13-17) to occur every year, three times a year (16:16)

1. Deuteronomy does not identify the place the Lord would choose. What place will God choose to dwell in Israel? See 2 Chron. 6:5-6 and Psalm 132:13-14.

2. What is Israel to present at the place of the Lord's choosing? See 12:5-7; 16:16-17.

> **Against Idolatry**
>
> Interspersed throughout the covenant stipulations, especially the first section, are several prohibitions against specific idolatrous practices. Some of the prohibitions would not make sense by themselves, but they are forbidden because of their association with contemporary idolatrous practices.
>
> - Sacrificing children (12:31; 18:9)
> - Drinking blood (12:16, 23; 15:23)
> - Self-mutilation (14:1)
> - Boiling a kid in mother's milk (14:21)
> - Planted trees as Asherah (16:21)
> - Pillars (16:22)
> - Divination (18:10-12)

3. What statements frame the dietary laws (14:2, 21)? What does this indicate about Israel's diet?

46

4. What kinds of animals and fish are considered clean according to 14:6, 9?

5. What reminder of Israel's experience is given in the law in Deut. 15:15; 16:12? How will this affect their practice in the new land?

6. What kind of sacrifices are prohibited according to 15:19-23. What does this instruction teach us about worship to God?

> "For you are a people holy to the Lord your God, and the Lord has chosen you to be a people for his treasured possession, out of all the peoples who are on the face of the earth" (14:2).

Sweeter Than Honey Deuteronomy

Lesson 9

The Covenant Laws, Part 2

Deuteronomy 12-26

History of the Covenant	Principles of the Covenant	Stipulations of the Covenant	Consequences of the Covenant	The Choice of the Covenant	Continuity of the Covenant
Deut. 1-4	Deut. 5-11	**Deut. 12-26**	Deut. 27-28	Deut. 29-30	Deut. 31-34
1st Speech	2nd Speech	2nd Speech	3rd Speech	3rd Speech	Epilogue

The first section is specifically related to worship and Israel's responsibilities to God. The remaining sections address many moral and civil matters, but the religious aspect of Israelite life is never left behind. All the laws should be obeyed in the context of the covenant with God, and they necessarily have a religious component to them.

The Content of the Covenant Laws (ch. 12-26)

Israel's Leaders (16:18-18:22)

The next section includes regulations on Israel's leaders including judges, kings, priests and prophets. A couple of sections provide transitions by considering two offices at a time (judge and priest in 17:8-13 and false priests and prophets in 18:9-14). The laws relate both to the proper function of the office and the people's acceptance of the decisions of the leaders.

Office	Appointment	Selected From	Summary of Instruction
Judges (16:18-17:13)	Appointed from people (16:18)	Each tribe (16:18)	- Judge righteously (16:18-20) - Stone idolaters (17:2-7) - Submit to decisions (17:8-13)
King (17:14-20)	Set by people; Chosen by God (17:15)	Among your Brothers (17:15)	- Selection of king (17:14-15) - Prohibited activities (17:16-17) - Reading the Law (17:18-20)
Priests (18:1-14)	Hereditary (18:1)	The Tribe of Levi (18:1)	- Provisions for priests (18:1-5) - Provision for Levites (18:6-8) - Forbidden practices (18:9-13)
Prophet (18:15-22)	Chosen by God (18:9)	Among your Brothers (18:15)	- God will raise a prophet to instruct the people (18:15-19) - Test for false prophet (18:20-22)

Sweeter Than Honey Deuteronomy

Judges, priests and prophets are familiar offices for Israel. The selection of judges occurred at Mt. Sinai (Ex. 18; Num. 11; Deut. 1:9-18) and many laws are devoted to the activities of the Levites and priests (Ex. 25 – Lev. 9). Moses and his siblings had served as prophets for the previous 40 years (Ex. 7:1; 15:20; Deut. 34:10; also see Num. 11:26-30). Kingship would be new, and Deuteronomy anticipates its establishment for the first time in the Law.

1. How are judges to conduct their job according to 16:18-20?

2. What is the king prohibited from doing? What is he commanded to do?

3. What kind of false religious practices are forbidden in 18:9-13?

4. Who will God raise up as a new prophet? See Deut. 34:9 and notice the irony of his words in Num. 11:26-30.

> "The Lord your God will raise up for you a prophet like me from among you, from among your brothers – it is to him you shall listen" (Deut. 18:15).

5. Who is the ultimate fulfillment of Moses' words according to Acts 3:17-26 and 7:37?

Lesson 9

Criminal and Military Justice (19:1-22:8)

The next section alternates between criminal matters and military matters. The criminal cases generally result in the loss of life like murder and manslaughter. The military instructions begin with a call to confidence before considering scenarios of victory. Military defeat is not considered in these instructions.

> "For the Lord your God is he who goes with you to fight for you against your enemies, to give you the victory" (Deut. 20:4).

- *Criminal*: Cities of Refuge (19:1-13) and Witnesses (19:15-21)
- *Military*: Courage in Battle (20:1-9) and Military Strategy (20:10-20)
- *Criminal*: Atonement for Murder (21:1-9)
- *Military*: Wives from War (21:10-14) and Favoritism in Polygamy (21:15-17)
- *Criminal*: Rebellious Sons (21:18-21), Burial for Criminals (21:22-23), Assorted Laws concluding with a roof parapet to avoid negligent manslaughter (22:1-8)

6. What will cause the Israelite army to fear their opposition? See 20:1.

7. Why are cities to be devoted to destruction? See 20:16-18.

8. Who is allowed to leave Israel's army? How could they be confident with reduced numbers?

Sweeter Than Honey Deuteronomy

Purity (22:9-23:18)

Laws about improper mixing introduce this section on purity before moving on to purity in marriage and the assembly. The laws about purity in marriage address situations involving a married or betrothed woman. The prohibition against adultery is taken seriously in the law, serving as one of the Ten Commandments and often resulting in the death penalty. Purity in Israel also involved excluded certain ones from the assembly and the camp.

> **Laws in Deut. 22:9-23:18**
> - Unlawful mixing (22:9-11)
> - Purity involving a Married or Betrothed Woman (22:12-30)
> - Exclusion from the Assembly (23:1-8)
> - Exclusion from the Camp (23:9-14)
> - Cult Prostitutes (23:17-18)

9. What three things should not be mixed according to 22:9-11?

10. Who is forbidden from the assembly of the Lord?

11. Why does Israel's camp need to be holy according to 23:14?

> **Purge the Evil from Your Midst.** The death penalty was the punishment for capital crimes such as murder, adultery and kidnapping. The motivation for its employment was to "purge the evil from your midst, a phrase which is found 11 times in the covenant stipulations (13:5; 17:7, 12; 19:13, 19; 21:9, 21; 22:21, 22, 24; 24:7).

Lesson 9

Interpersonal Affairs (23:19-25:19)

A large variety of laws can be found in this section under the general heading of interpersonal affairs, or how Israelites relate to others in society. The laws particularly consider just practices regarding economics and the poor (see (23:19-20; 24:1-4; 10-15, 17-22; 25:13-16).

> **Laws in Deut. 23:19-25:19**
> - Charging Interest (23:19-20)
> - Vows (23:21-23)
> - Eating from another's field (23:24-25)
> - Divorce (24:1-4)
> - Military leave for newly married (24:5)
> - Proper pledges (24:6)
> - Kidnapping (24:7)
> - Lepers (24:8-13)
> - Oppressing the poor (24:14-15)
> - Punishment for guilty (24:16)
> - Proper pledges (24:17-18)
> - Food provisions for poor (24:19-22)
> - Punishment in disputes (25:1-3)
> - Muzzling an ox (25:4)
> - Levirate marriage (25:5-10)
> - Hitting below the belt (25:11-12)
> - Just weights (25:13-16)
> - Defeating the Amalekites (25:17-19)

12. Why is charging interest prohibited?

13. Why is the law on divorce given in 24:1-4? Who does it protect?

14. What provisions are made for the poor in 24:19-22?

15. What do these laws such as 24:16 and 25:1-3 teach about just punishments?

16. What is Israel to do to the Amalekites? Why?

53

Sweeter Than Honey Deuteronomy

Covenant Remembrance (26:1-15)

The final section concludes with instructions for two separate offerings already discussed: firstfruits (26:1-11; 16:9-12) and the third-year tithe (26:12-15; 14:22-29). The offerings are brought in worship to God, and each one concludes with a prayer (v. 10, 15). On both occasions, the Israelite is molded into a gracious giver by reflecting on God as a gracious giver.

17. Identify God's provision. Identify what and to whom the Israelite gift is given.

Occasion	God's Provision	Israelite Act of Giving
Firstfruits (v. 1-11)		
Third Year Tithe (v. 12-15)		

Conclusion (26:16-19)

The stipulations conclude with an exhortation, which serves to bracket the covenant stipulations (12:1; 26:16) and declarations (26:17-19). Moses urges careful obedience before considering the covenant commitments of the Lord and the people.

18. Identify what the people declare and what the Lord declares.

The People (26:17)	The Lord (26:18-19)
1.	
2.	
3.	
4.	

Lesson 10

Blessings and Curses
Deuteronomy 27-28

History of the Covenant	Principles of the Covenant	Stipulations of the Covenant	**Consequences of the Covenant**	The Choice of the Covenant	Continuity of the Covenant
Deut. 1-4	Deut. 5-11	Deut. 12-26	**Deut. 27-28**	Deut. 29-30	Deut. 31-34
1ˢᵗ Speech	2ⁿᵈ Speech			3ʳᵈ Speech	Epilogue

Renewing the Covenant (27:1-28:68)

Chapters 27-28 conclude the 2ⁿᵈ speech of Moses, providing a fitting conclusion to the covenant stipulations. This text records the elements of the ceremony, which includes the following items:

- Writing the law for display on large stones.
- Building an altar to sacrifice to the Lord.
- Eating a covenant meal.
- Reciting the consequences (blessings and curses) of the covenant.

> "Keep silence and hear, O Israel: this day you have become the people of the LORD your God" (Deut. 27:9).

The ceremony will take place "in the land" (27:2), and it is celebrated under the leadership of Joshua after the victories over Jericho and Ai (Josh. 8:30-35).

Display the Law (27:2-4, 8)

Moses instructs the people to set up large stones in the land and write the laws of the covenant upon them, suggesting both their permanence and accessibility. It was common practice in the Ancient Near East to display the law of the land on stone in a public place. Plaster covers the stones before writing, which was borrowed from Egyptian practice. In contrast, the people of Mesopotamia and Canaan carved into stone rather than using plaster.

In verse 8, Moses commands the words of the law to be written "plainly," echoing the first section of the book where Moses spoke "plainly," explaining them to make them clear.

"Beyond the Jordan, in the land of Moab, Moses undertook to explain (Hebrew bā'ar) this law" (1:5)	"And you shall write on the stones all the words of this law very plainly (Hebrew bā'ar)" (27:8)

Sweeter Than Honey Deuteronomy

1. What is the advantage of displaying the law in a public place?

2. What does it mean to write the laws plainly?

Sacrifice to the Lord (27:5-6)

Next, Moses commands the people to build an altar to offer sacrifices. The construction of the altar follows the instructions from Ex. 20:22-26. The altar would serve the purpose of sacrifices for the covenant ceremony, with both burnt offerings and peace offerings being used. The burnt offerings totally consumed the sacrifice and are offered "to the LORD your God" (v. 6).

3. What kind of stones are to be used to build the altar? Why is this instruction given?

Eat a Covenant Meal (27:7)

While burnt offerings are totally consumed, there would be meat left over from a peace offering. This sacrifice engendered peace among the people as they sacrificed together, ate the leftover meat together, and rejoiced "before the LORD your God" (v. 7).

4. The people are all making a covenant with God. What does this mean for their relationship together? How is their relationship together changed because of their relationship with God?

Recite the Blessings and Curses (27:9-28:68)

The bulk of the instructions on the ceremony relate to the consequences of the covenant. To recite the consequences, Moses divides the people into two groups, one on Mount Gerizim to represent the blessings and one on Mount Ebal to represent the curses. The Levites announced the consequences and the people responded with "Amen" to declare their agreement.

Mt. Gerizim (Blessings)	Mt. Ebal (Curses)
Simeon	Reuben
Levi	Gad
Judah	Asher
Issachar	Zebulun
Joseph	Dan
Benjamin	Naphtali

The consequences underscore the importance of covenant faithfulness. Obedience yields blessings while disobedience results in curses. Israel's affirmation of the consequences is a way of binding themselves to the covenant.

> Curses for Disobedience (27:15-26)
> Blessings for Obedience (28:1-14)
> Curses for Disobedience (28:15-68)

There are three groups of consequences named. A section of blessings is sandwiched between two groups of curses. The opening section of curses is distinct from consequences announced in chapter 28.

Curses (ch. 27)

The first section identifies the type of sins that will bring a curse upon people without specifying the kind of curse that will come. Twelve curses are given, and some of the sins can be grouped together into categories.

5. Identify the type of sins that bring a curse below.

   Idolatry 1)

   Family 2)

   3)

   Justice 4)

   5)

   6)

   7)

   Sexual 8)

   9)

   10)

   Violence 11)

   Obedience 12)

6. Identify Mt. Gerizim and Mt. Ebal on a map.

7. How do the people respond to these curses?

8. Why do you think these sins are identified?

9. How does someone "confirm" the law according to the last curse?

Blessed shall you be... (28:3-6)

In the city
In the field
In the fruit of your womb
In the fruit of the ground
In the fruit of livestock
In your basket and kneading bowl
When you come and when you go

Cursed shall you be... (28:16-19)

Blessings and Curses (ch. 28)

The blessings and curses of chapter 28 are two sides of the same coin. They represent a mirror image of one another. The blessings are the good things that will come upon Israel by means of God's grace through their obedience. They relate to the fundamental wants and needs of the people, which produce happiness and fulfillment in the Lord. The curses are a removal of the blessings, resulting in misery and despair. The close connection between the blessings and curses can be seen in the use of similar language in Deuteronomy 28:3-6, 16-19. Blessings and curses can be found in other passages throughout Deuteronomy and the Pentateuch (Lev. 26; Deut. 4, 30, 32). In general, the blessings and curses can be divided into common themes and categories.

Categories of the Blessings and Curses

Blessings	Curses
Life and Peace	Terror and Dread
Victory over Enemies	Defeat before Enemies
Esteem	Contempt
Possession of the Land	Exile from the Land
Health	Sickness and Disease
Children	Barrenness
Livestock	Livestock
Agriculture	Agriculture

10. Why do you think more curses are listed than blessings?

11. What impression does this chapter leave on you? What emotions does it stir?

12. What role does Egypt play in the curses? Why does God reference that nation?

The instructions for the covenant ceremony resemble the ceremony at Sinai in Exodus 24. The original ceremony was celebrated by Moses, Aaron, Nadab, Abihu and the 70 elders. In contrast, this covenant is to be celebrated among all the people.

Covenant Ceremony (Exodus 24)	Renewal Ceremony (Deut. 27-28)
Moses built an altar (24:4)	Build an altar (27:5-6)
Twelve pillars erected (24:4)	Erect stones to write the law (27:2-4)
Burnt and Peace offerings made (24:5)	Offer burnt and peace offerings (27:6-7)
They "beheld God, ate and drank" (24:9-11)	Eat a covenant meal together (27:7)

13. What differences exist between the two covenant ceremonies?

Sweeter Than Honey Deuteronomy

Lesson 11

Israel's Choice

Deuteronomy 29-30

History of the Covenant	Principles of the Covenant	Stipulations of the Covenant	Consequences of the Covenant	**The Choice of the Covenant**	Continuity of the Covenant
Deut. 1-4	Deut. 5-11	Deut. 12-26	Deut. 27-28	**Deut. 29-30**	Deut. 31-34
1st Speech	2nd Speech			3rd Speech	Epilogue

Overview (29:1)

"These are the words of the covenant that the LORD commanded Moses to make with the people of Israel in the land of Moab, besides the covenant that he had made with them at Horeb" (29:1).

The first verse (29:1) establishes the setting, referencing Israel's covenant with God at Moab. The third and final speech of Moses, found in Deuteronomy 29-30, provides a natural progression through the book. Moses has outlined the covenant for the people, including the historical context (ch. 1-4), the principles and reasons for obedience (ch. 5-11), the specific stipulations or laws (ch. 12-26) and the consequences of obedience or disobedience (ch. 27-28).

Now the choice to obey or disobey is left with Israel. In this section, Moses reviews some of the history before declaring the two paths that lay before Israel – obedience and disobedience. Neither path is predetermined, and the people have the opportunity to change course at any time.

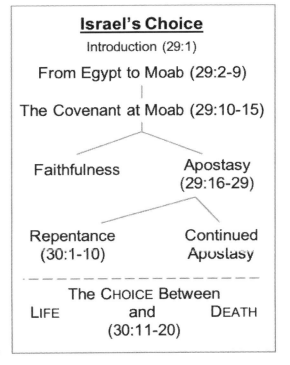

Sweeter Than Honey Deuteronomy

The Covenant Context (29:2-15)

Moses first summarizes what Israel has witnessed God accomplish from Egypt to Moab (29:2-9), bringing them to their current situation of the covenant (29:10-15).

1. Identify what Israel has witnessed at each place:
   a. Egypt (v. 2-3)

   b. The Wilderness (v. 4-6)

   c. Transjordan (v. 7-8)

2. What does verse 4 mean by stating that "the LORD has not given you a heart to understand or eyes to see or ears to hear"?

3. What should Israel have learned from their experience according to verse 6?

Moses moves from their history to the current situation in Moab where the people are making a covenant with God (29:10-15). In this section Moses stresses the participants and the purpose of the covenant.

4. Who are identified as the covenant participants?

5. What is the purpose of the covenant according to v. 13?

Lesson 11

The Choice Between Life and Death (29:16-30:20)

Now that the covenant has been made, Israel has a choice to make about whether they will honor it or disregard it, whether they will live faithfully or in apostasy. Moses examines these choices by considering two scenarios: what happens if they choose to fall away from the Lord (29:16-29) and what happens when they repent in the midst of apostasy (30:1-10). With the consequences of their choices in mind, Moses calls upon the people to make the choice, to choose between life and death (30:11-20).

The Path of Apostasy (29:16-29)

Moses begins with a warning, telling the people to beware of falling away from the Lord. The section contains three parts with a concluding, transition verse.
- The Idolatry of the Nations around Them (v. 16-17)
- Warning Against Falling Away from the Lord (v. 18-19)
- The Consequences of Apostasy (v. 20-28)
- The Secret Things of the Lord (v. 29)

"Beware lest there be among you a man or woman or clan or tribe whose heart is turning away from the LORD our God to serve the gods of those nations" (29:18).

Having examined the potential influence of Israel's idolatrous nations, Moses warns Israel lest anyone's "heart is turning away from the LORD our God to serve the gods of those nations." Then he outlines some consequences of this particular choice.

6. How does Moses describe the idols in v. 17?

7. What kind of self-deception does Moses warn against? What kind of "root" is described in this warning?

8. What will happen to the one who falls from the Lord?

Sweeter Than Honey Deuteronomy

9. Note the nations' charge and the response given below.

The Nations' Charge:	The People's Response:

10. Who are the "people" who respond to the nations in 29:25-28?

Deut. 29:29 states, *"The secret things belong to the LORD our God, but the things that are revealed belong to us and to our children forever, that we may do all the words of this law."* This verse contrasts the unknown vs. the revealed things of God.

11. Why is this verse given here? Does it relate to the previous or next sections?

The Path of Repentance (30:1-10)

The second scenario to be considered is the path of repentance. When Israel suffers the consequences of apostasy and recalls the words of the covenant in exile in a foreign land, they may repent and turn to the Lord. This section mirrors the talk of renewal after judgment in Leviticus 26:40-45, which is provided there in the context of the blessings and curses.

> **Structure in Deut. 30:1-10**
>
> Scenario established (v. 1)
> **A.** When you turn and obey with your heart and soul (v. 2)
>   **B.** The Lord will prosper you (v. 3-5)
>   **C.** The Lord will circumcise your heart so that you love God with all your heart and soul (v. 6)
>   **B'.** The Lord will prosper you (v. 7-9)
> **A'.** When you obey and turn with your heart and soul (v. 10)

The passage is structured according to a chiasm or concentric pattern. The outer most sections repeat the key concepts of Israel's turning and obeying. The next adjacent sections speak of the benefit of repentance; the Lord will gather them from captivity and prosper them. The central, prominent section pictures a circumcision of Israel's heart so that they love God with all their heart and soul.

The section is filled with repetitions that help to underscore the point.
- Return or turn (Hebrew *shoov*) occurs 7 times (not all of which are discernable in an English translation; "return to mind" in v. 1; "return" or "repent" in v. 2, 8, 10; "restore" in v. 3; "again" as in "gather again" in v. 3 and "delight again" in v. 9.

Lesson 11

- "With all your heart and with all your soul" occurs 3 times, in the two outer sections and the central section.
- "the LORD your God" occurs 12 times, and it consists of God's personal, covenant name and the possessive "your" to emphasize the nation's relationship to God.

12. What actions are the people responsible for in this passage? What about the Lord?

13. What does it mean that the Lord will circumcise their heart? What is involved?

Choose Life or Death (30:11-20)

Moses demonstrates the possibility and accessibility of obedience (v. 11-14) before setting the two choices of life and death clearly before the people (v. 15-20). Obedience of the covenant is not an impossible task but an attainable goal, available to any who desired to do it. Not only is it possible, but it is needful and good to obey. When life and death are the options, the choice of life is obviously the recommended path. *"Therefore choose life, that you and your offspring may live…"* (v. 19b).

> "See, I have set before you today life and good, death and evil" (v. 15).

14. What imagery does Moses use to demonstrate the nearness of the command?

15. Identify the conditions and consequences of the choices of life and death.

The Choice of Life (30:16)	The Choice of Death (30:17-18)
If…	If…
Then…	Then…

16. Who does Moses call as witnesses of the covenant and its consequences?

17. What does it mean to choose life according to verse 20?

Lesson 12

Witnesses to the Covenant

Deuteronomy 31-32

History of the Covenant	Principles of the Covenant	Stipulations of the Covenant	Consequences of the Covenant	The Choice of the Covenant	Continuity of the Covenant
Deut. 1-4	Deut. 5-11	Deut. 12-26	Deut. 27-28	Deut. 29-30	**Deut. 31-34**
1st Speech	2nd Speech			3rd Speech	**Epilogue**

Epilogue (chapters 31-34)

Deuteronomy 30 concludes the third and final speech of Moses to Israel with the last four chapters forming the epilogue (Deut. 31-34). The epilogue provides the narrative conclusion to Deuteronomy, providing the final words of Moses along with the account of his death and the transition of power to Joshua. It also forms a frame around the book with the opening chapters. Deuteronomy 1-4 tells the history of Israel from Sinai up until when Moses gives the speeches of Deuteronomy. The epilogue picks up at the conclusion of Moses' speeches and concludes the narrative.

Outline of the Epilogue

Addresses from Moses (31:1-13)
At the Tent of Meeting (31:14-23)
Storage of the Covenant (31:24-29)
The Song of Moses (31:30-32:43)
Moses' Charge to Israel (32:44-47)
God Predicts Moses' Death (32:48-52)
Moses Blesses Israel (33:1-29)
The Death of Moses (34:1-8)
Joshua Assumes Leadership (34:9-12)

> "The LORD your God himself will go over before you. He will destroy these nations before you, so that you shall dispossess them, and Joshua will go over at your head, as the LORD has spoken" (v. 3).

Speeches to the People (31:1-29)

Deuteronomy 31 consists of a series of speeches made by Moses and the Lord. The messages address the task of entering the land while being faithful to the covenant of God, and they are made in light of the transition of leadership that will soon take place. What Moses began by leading the people out of Egypt, Joshua will complete by leading the people into Canaan.

1. Summarize the basic message given to each group of people.

Moses Addresses the People (31:1-6)	God summons Moses and Joshua (31:14-15)
	God Addresses Moses concerning the People (31:16-18)
Moses Addresses Joshua (31:7-8)	Moses commanded to write the song (31:19-22)
	God Addresses Joshua (31:23)
Moses Addresses the Levites (31:9-13)	Moses Addresses the Levites (31:24-29)

Witnesses to the Covenant

Covenants are legal and binding agreements, and provisions are put in place to verify and validate the agreement and its terms. A written document is created and stored for future reference, and witnesses attest to their truthfulness. Both of the elements emphasize the seriousness and enduring nature of the agreement being made.

Three separate witnesses can be found in Deuteronomy 31: 1) heaven and earth, 2) the book of the covenant, and 3) the song of Moses. Typically, people serve as witnesses and can validate a message with their speech. None of the witnesses in this chapter are the typical human witness, but they still provide testimony of the covenant.

Witness #1: Heaven and Earth (31:28)

Moses calls upon heaven and earth to be a witness to the covenant. This makes the third time in the book that Moses has called upon the physical creation to serve as a witness (4:26; 30:19; see also 32:1).

2. Why do you think heaven and earth are chosen as witnesses for Israel's covenant with God?

Lesson 12

Witness #2: The Book of the Covenant (31:26)

After writing the Law down, provision is made for its storage and routine reading. The Law is to be stored in the Ark of the Covenant, and it will serve as a continual witness of the covenant for generations to come.

> "Take this Book of the Law and put it by the side of the ark of the covenant of the Lord your God, that it may be there for a witness against you" (v. 26).

3. When is the law to be read before the people?

4. How can the book of the law serve as a witness?

Witness #3: The Song of Moses (31:19, 21)

> "Now therefore write this song and teach it to the people of Israel. Put it in their mouths, that this song may be a witness for me against the people of Israel" (v. 19).

The Lord delivers some sad news to Moses in one of his final conversations (31:16-22). After Moses dies, Israel will fall away from the Lord. For this reason, God instructs Moses to write down the song and teach it to the people. The Song of Moses, which is recorded in Deuteronomy 32, serves as a witness for the people in the face of their disobedience.

5. What is the purpose of this song? What will it accomplish for future generations?

6. What role should God's word play for the people?

7. What does this chapter teach about the need to repeatedly hear God's word?

69

The Song of Moses (31:30-32:47)

A Lawsuit Against Israel (32:1-25)

The song that Moses is instructed to write (31:19) appears in Deuteronomy 32:1-43. The first part of the poem closely resembles the form of a treaty lawsuit from the Ancient Near East. This type of lawsuit provided the means for a lord to bring charges against a vassal for breaking the covenant. The lawsuit including the following elements, all of which can be found in the first part of the Song of Moses:
- Call of Witnesses
- Statement of Master's Benevolence
- Accusation
- Evidence of Covenant Violation
- Announcement of Punishment

Structure of the Song of Moses
1. The Opening Declaration and Call of Witnesses (v. 1-3)
2. The Lord's Faithfulness and Israel's Unfaithfulness (v. 4-9)
3. The Lord's Provision for Israel (v. 10-14)
4. The Indictment of Israel's Apostasy (v. 15-18)
5. The Sentence (v. 19-25)
6. The Lord Deliberates the Sentence (v. 26-35)
7. The Lord Vindicates Himself and Saves His People (v. 35-43)

The lawsuit structure is a common feature of the prophets, and it is found in Hosea 4:1-6; Micah 6:1-5, and Jeremiah 2:4-13.

8. Who are the witnesses of the lawsuit against Israel?

9. What image is used to portray God in verse 4? What kind of character does he have?

10. What accusation does the Lord bring against Israel?

11. What sentence does Israel deserve?

The Sentence Reconsidered (32:26-43)

What makes this poem so extraordinary is the continuation of the song after the lawsuit. A full resolution to the lawsuit comes in verse 25 with a guilty verdict and a national death sentence. However, when God considers such an end for his people, he cannot carry out the sentence. Instead, he determines to "vindicate his people and have compassion on his servants" (v. 36). By extending grace and compassion, God demonstrates that he is unique and the one true God. The poem concludes with a doxology in verse 43 as the witnesses of the lawsuit gives praise to God (v. 1, 43).

> God: "See now that I, even I, am he, and there is no god beside me" (v. 39a)

12. How will the Lord "vindicate" his people?

13. What does this poem teach about God? How does this fit in with the theme of Deuteronomy?

Conclusion (32:44-52)

Chapter 32 contains a narrative conclusion with a final charge from Moses (v. 44-47) and the Lord's instruction to ascend Mt. Nebo to view the land of Canaan and die on the mountain (v. 48-52).

14. What final charge does Moses give to Israel? What is at stake?

Sweeter Than Honey Deuteronomy

Lesson 13

The Final Days of Moses
Deuteronomy 33-34

History of the Covenant	Principles of the Covenant	Stipulations of the Covenant	Consequences of the Covenant	The Choice of the Covenant	**Continuity of the Covenant**
Deut. 1-4	Deut. 5-11	Deut. 12-26	Deut. 27-28	Deut. 29-30	**Deut. 31-34**
1st Speech	2nd Speech			3rd Speech	**Epilogue**

The final scene of Moses' life is recorded in the last two chapters of Deuteronomy, providing a transition for the nation of Israel and their ensuing history in the land of Canaan. God has just instructed him to ascend Mount Nebo (32:48-52) to the place he will die. Moses remains a leader to the end, blessing the people of Israel with his dying words (ch. 33) and transferring leadership to Joshua before his death (ch. 34).

Moses Blesses the Israelites (ch. 33)

With his final message Moses blesses the children of Israel, reminiscent of the blessings given by Isaac (Gen. 27:1-40) and Jacob (Gen. 49). The blessings particularly resemble Jacob's blessings with the same subjects identified. Whereas Jacob blessed his sons, Moses blesses their tribal descendants. Unlike Jacob's blessings, there are only positive blessings given by Moses.

> **Jeshurun** appears to be a synonymous reference to Israel, although the Hebrew word has an uncertain meaning. It is found only four times in Scripture, with three of those references found in a two-chapter span of Deuteronomy (Deut. 32:15; 33:5, 26; Isa. 44:2).

Structure of the Blessings of Moses (Deut. 33)	
Introduction (v. 1-5)	
Reuben (v. 6) Judah (v. 7) Levi (v. 8-11) Benjamin (v. 12) Joseph (v. 13-17)	Zebulun and Issachar (v. 18-19) Gad (v. 20-21) Dan (v. 22) Naphtali (v. 23) Asher (v. 24-25)
Conclusion (v. 26-29)	

Sweeter Than Honey Deuteronomy

The blessings are bracketed by an introduction (v. 1-5) and a conclusion (v. 26-29), which establish the basis of blessings and summarize the main themes. These sections are also tied together by references to Jeshurun, another name for Israel (v. 5, 26). The central section contains ten separate blessings (v. 6-25) that expand upon the benefits of the covenant already discussed in Deuteronomy. The half-tribes of Ephraim and Manasseh are included under the blessing for Joseph. Zebulun and Issachar are combined, and Simeon is omitted. Levi and Joseph receive the longest blessings with each occupying at least four verses. The blessing for Levi is unique in that it considers past events while describing the special purpose for the tribe. Joseph's blessing provides the fullest description.

The introduction and conclusion establish the basis of Israel's blessings. God is a loving and powerful God, and the source of all blessings. Israel's relationship with him through continued covenant loyalty provides access to these blessings. Two blessings in particular are mentioned in the final address of Moses: victory over enemies and good life in the land. The conclusion summarizes these themes in a clear and straightforward way by extolling the uniqueness of God and his covenant people Israel.

Conclusion: Summary of Blessings (33:26-29)

1. What three locations are mentioned in the introduction?

2. How does the introduction describe the relationship between God and Israel?

3. Which tribes are blessed with victory/protection and good life in the land?

Tribe	Victory/ Protection	Good Life in the Land	Notes
Reuben (v. 6)			
Judah (v. 7)			
Levi (v. 8-11)			
Benjamin (v. 12)			
Joseph (v. 13-17)			
Zebulun and Issachar (v. 18-19)			
Gad (v. 20-21)			
Dan (v. 22)			
Naphtali (v. 23)			
Asher (v. 24-25)			

4. Why do you think Simeon is omitted from the blessings?

5. What purpose is ascribed to Levi?

6. How are Joseph's blessings in the land described? What kind of military victory will he have?

7. How is God depicted in the introduction? How is God depicted in the conclusion?

The Death of Moses (ch. 34)

For the first 33 chapters in Deuteronomy, Moses has been the primary speaker as he exhorted Israel to be loyal to God and his covenant. In the final chapter, he does not speak. His voice is silent as he faces his death on top of the mountain. The only speech in the chapter comes from the Lord, who shows Moses the land before commenting on it.

The chapter contains the following structure:

- The Lord shows Moses the land (v. 1-4)
- Moses dies and is buried (v. 5-7)
- Joshua succeeds Moses (v. 9)
- Reflection on the life of Moses (v. 10-12)

Moses, the Mountain Climber

Moses was an accomplished mountain climber, and it is fitting that the mountaintop is his final destination.

- He climbs **Mount Sinai/ Horeb** 6-8 times in order to receive the law from God (Ex. 19-20, 24, 32-34).
- He climbs **Mount Hor** to witness the death of Aaron (Num. 20:27).
- He climbs **Mount Nebo** to view the land of Canaan before his death (Deut. 34:1-3).

Deuteronomy 34 provides the conclusion for many different elements, including the book of Deuteronomy and the Pentateuch story. Moses is the main character during pivotal periods of Israel's history, which are mentioned here: their deliverance from Egyptian bondage (v. 11), their covenant with God at Mt. Sinai (v. 10), and their journey in the wilderness (v. 12) to the Promised Land of Canaan (v. 4).

The chapter also concludes the story of the disobedience and punishment of Moses and Aaron. Aaron faced his death by ascending Mt. Hor and transferring the priestly leadership to his son Eleazar. Similar preparations are made for Moses, which are carried out in Deuteronomy 34.

Transition of Leadership

Aaron → Eleazar
Moses → Joshua

Moses' and Aaron's Sin and Punishment	Aaron's Death	Preparations for Moses' Death	Moses' Death
Num. 20:2-13	Num. 20:22-29	Num. 27:12-23 Deut. 32:48-52	Deut. 34:1-8

Other references to the death of Moses: Deut. 3:23-29; 31:1-2; 33:1

This final chapter contains references to some unspecified future date, stating that no one knows the site of Moses' burial "to this day" (v. 6) and no one has arisen like him "since" that time (v. 10). Most of the book contains the final speeches of Moses, while this chapter provides the narrative conclusion and reflection on his life.

Lesson 13

8. Where is Moses buried?

9. What provision does God give Moses in the midst of his punishment?

10. How is Moses' health described at his death?

11. Who succeeds Moses, and how is he described?

12. What roles does Moses play during his life for the people of Israel?

13. How is Moses unique in Israel's history?

Sweeter Than Honey Deuteronomy

Review

Deuteronomy 1-34

History of the Covenant	Principles of the Covenant	Stipulations of the Covenant	Consequences of the Covenant	The Choice of the Covenant	Continuity of the Covenant
Deut. 1-4	Deut. 5-11	Deut. 12-26	Deut. 27-28	Deut. 29-30	Deut. 31-34
1st Speech	2nd Speech			3rd Speech	Epilogue

1. What is the setting for the book of Deuteronomy? What has the nation just finished doing and what are they preparing to do in the near future?

2. How is the book of Deuteronomy structured?

3. How does Deuteronomy resemble a covenant? What covenant components are in the book?

4. What does the book reveal about the character of God?

5. What implications does God's character have for God's people and how they should act?

6. What is wrong with idolatry? Why is it so severely condemned?

7. How are the Ten Commandments different than the rest of the Law? What function does it perform for Israel?

8. How are God's requirements for Israel the same as what he requires from his people today? How is it different?

9. What role does history play in the book?

10. How does this book stress the importance of obedience?

11. What are the consequences of obedience? What are the consequences of disobedience?

12. How and in what way is Israel to love the Lord?

13. How important is teaching the next generation? In what ways should a parent teach their child?

14. What kind of temptations would Israel face when they enjoyed the bounty of the land? How does this apply to today?

15. What does the study of Deuteronomy reveal about the function and importance of preaching?

16. Deuteronomy has been called "the gospel according to Moses." In what ways does the message of Deuteronomy correspond with the gospel ultimately revealed in Christ?

17. What does this book show us about Moses as a leader?

18. Is there anything else that impressed you about Deuteronomy? What else did you learn?

Resources

Works Cited

Block, Daniel I. *The NIV Application Commentary: Deuteronomy*. Edited by Terry Muck. Grand Rapids, MI: Zondervan, 2012.

Craigie, Peter C. *The Book of Deuteronomy*. The New International Commentary on the Old Testament. Grand Rapids, MI: Wm. B. Eerdmans Publishing Co., 1976.

Merrill, Eugene H. *Deuteronomy*. Vol. 4. The New American Commentary. Nashville: Broadman & Holman Publishers, 1994.

Some Other Helpful Resources

Hamilton, Victor P. *Handbook on the Pentateuch*. 2nd ed. Grand Rapids, MI: Baker Academic, 2005.

McConville, J. G. *Deuteronomy*. Edited by David W. Baker and Gordon J. Wenham. Vol. 5. Apollos Old Testament Commentary. Leicester, England; Downers Grove, IL: Apollos; InterVarsity Press, 2002.

Miller, Patrick D. *Deuteronomy*. Interpretation, a Bible Commentary for Teaching and Preaching. Louisville, KY: J. Knox Press, 1990.

Tigay, Jeffrey H. *Deuteronomy*. The JPS Torah Commentary. Philadelphia: Jewish Publication Society, 1996.

Wright, Christopher J. H. *Deuteronomy*. Edited by W. Ward Gasque, Robert L. Hubbard Jr., and Robert K. Johnston. Understanding the Bible Commentary Series. Grand Rapids, MI: Baker Books, 2012.

Made in the USA
Middletown, DE
07 September 2023